AMAZING WORLD WAR II STORIES

U.S. GHOST ARMY

THE MASTER ILLUSIONISTS
OF WORLD WAR II

by Nel Yomtov
illustrated by Alessandro Valdrighi

Consultant:
Tim Solie
Adjunct Professor of History
Minnesota State University, Mankato
Mankato, Minnesota

CAPSTONE PRESS
a capstone imprint

Graphic Library is published by Capstone Press,
1710 Roe Crest Drive, North Mankato, Minnesota 56003
www.capstonepub.com

Library of Congress Cataloging-in-Publication data
Names: Yomtov, Nelson, author. | Valdrighi, Alessandro, illustrator.
Title: U.S. Ghost Army : the master illusionists of World War II / by Nel Yomtov ;
  illustrated by Alessandro Valdrighi.
Other titles: Master illusionists of World War II
Description: North Mankato, Minnesota : Capstone Press, [2020] | Series: Graphic library.
  Amazing World War II stories | Includes bibliographical references and index. | Audience:
  Grades 4–6. | Audience: Ages 8–14.
Identifiers: LCCN 2019005964 (print) | LCCN 2019010352 (ebook) | ISBN 9781543573206
  (eBook PDF) | ISBN 9781543573169 (library binding) | ISBN 9781543575514 (paperback)
Subjects: LCSH: United States. Army. Headquarters Special Troops, 23rd—History—Juvenile
  literature. | World War, 1939–1945—Campaigns—Western Front—Juvenile literature. |
  World War, 1939–1945—Deception—United States—Juvenile literature. | Deception (Military
  science)—Juvenile literature.
Classification: LCC D769.25 (ebook) | LCC D769.25 .Y66 2020 (print) |
  DDC 940.54/8673—dc23
LC record available at https://lccn.loc.gov/2019005964

Summary: In graphic novel format, tells the amazing story of the U.S. Ghost Army and the vital
role it played in helping achieve successful missions in Europe during World War II.

EDITOR
Aaron J. Sautter

ART DIRECTOR
Nathan Gassman

DESIGNER
Ted Williams

PRODUCTION SPECIALIST
Katy LaVigne

Design Elements by Shutterstock/Guenter Albers

All internet sites appearing in back matter were available and accurate when this book was sent
to press.

Direct quotations appear in **_bold italicized text_** on the following pages:
Page 7: from *Ghost Army of World War II*, by Rick Beyer and Elizabeth Sayles. New York:
  Princeton Architectural Press, 2015.
Page 10: from *Secret Soldiers: The Story of World War II's Heroic Army of Deception*,
  by Philip Gerard. New York: Dutton, 2002.
Page 29: from *Ghost Army of World War II*, by Jack Kneece. Gretna, LA: Pelican Pub. Co., 2001.

Printed in the United States   6000

TABLE OF CONTENTS

MASTERS OF DECEPTION

In January 1944, the United States Army created a new, one-of-a-kind unit called the 23rd Headquarters Special Troops. The unit was formed to deceive and confuse German troops in Europe during World War II (1939–1945).

The unit's main mission was to trick the Germans into believing the U.S. military had more forces in Europe than it actually had.

The Special Troops acted as a decoy while the real units operated elsewhere. They used unique equipment for their missions including inflatable rubber tanks, jeeps, and artillery. The unit also created fake sonic and radio broadcasts to trick German forces.

The unit included many creative people such as artists, writers, actors, and even fashion designers. In all, the 23rd Headquarters Special Troops included 1,100 men.

Members of the Special Troops trained at various camps in the United States. Meanwhile, American companies designed and built the unit's unique equipment.

In May 1944 most of the men in the 23rd sailed to England aboard the USS *Henry Gibbons* to join the war in Europe. By now, the special unit had earned a mysterious nickname: the Ghost Army.

From April 1944 to June 1945, the Ghost Army took part in 21 missions. The unit participated in some of the biggest and most important battles of the war.

Germany

Berlin

Netherlands

Great Britain

London

Belgium

Brussels

4. Operation Viersen:
Rhine River, Germany,
March 18–24, 1945

Luxembourg

Paris

1. Operation Elephant:
St. Lô, France,
July 1–4, 1944

3. Operation Metz:
Metz, France,
December 28–31, 1944

2. Operation Brittany:
Brest, France,
August 20–27, 1944

France

Switzerland

Using their talents and skills, the men in the Ghost Army had a huge impact on the outcome of the war. In the process, they would become the greatest group of con artists in military history.

Spain

Italy

GROWING PAINS

June 6, 1944, is best known as D-Day. Nearly 160,000 Allied troops landed on beaches along France's Normandy region. By the end of the month, 850,000 men had landed.

The Allies' first challenge was to break through the stiff German resistance in Normandy. At the end of June, the Ghost Army was given its first real test in Operation Elephant.

We've been ordered to move out immediately.

We're to play the part of the 2nd Armored Division in the Cerisy Forest. The real division will move to the battle line further ahead near Cherbourg.

Orders on such short notice? How can we organize an effective deception? The sonic unit is still training in England.

No matter. If we're successful, the German tanks won't move at all. They'll be focused on us . . .

. . . and believe we're the real 2nd Armored Division.

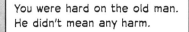

You were hard on the old man. He didn't mean any harm.

Many of the local people work as spies for the Germans. Any break in security could ruin the operation. It could mean death for us all in the Ghost Army.

We've got to be careful.

The Ghost Army held their position for three days. They continued their deception until the 3rd Armored Division moved in to relieve them. On July 4, the dummy equipment was deflated and packed away for the next mission.

Meanwhile, the Germans had made no attempt to follow the real U.S. forces on their way to Cherbourg. A short while later, Allied forces captured the city from the Germans.

The mission had been successful. However, the Ghost Army troops knew they'd gotten lucky. As they moved through the bombed-out city of St. Lô, France, they discussed Operation Elephant.

A lot was wrong with that mission. We got our orders the same day the 2nd Armored pulled out. We had no time to scout the area or plan a good deception.

Our vehicles weren't even painted correctly. They didn't have the markings on the bumpers of the 2nd Armored vehicles.

And we should have worn the same shoulder patches as the units we were imitating.

Our job is to convince everyone--including the Germans and the local people. They all need to think we're really the unit we're mimicking.

I wonder what the top brass will have to say about our "performance."

Yeah, I can't wait for the reviews to come in.

Lieutenant Fred Fox was the first officer to evaluate the Ghost Army's performance in Operation Elephant.

As commander of the Ghost Army, Colonel Reeder, you must know . . . *there is too much military--and not enough showmanship.*

This is bad theater . . . They must repair "tanks," hang out washing, and generally mill around in typical GI style.

Our radio operators are trained to imitate real operators using Morse code. We must use radio messages to provide false information. This will deceive the Germans when they intercept our radio traffic.

I read you loud and clear, Colonel. Consider it done.

From that point on, the Ghost Army wore the patches of the units they impersonated. Sometimes the patches were borrowed, other times they were created by the soldiers.

Good thing I learned to sew in high school!

Special Troops often pretended to be from real units as they moved within towns. They even mingled with the locals. They spread false information about their unit's strength and plans.

We've got a whole battalion camped just five miles from here!

Sometimes Ghost Army soldiers even impersonated high-ranking U.S. officers. They hoped to convince enemy spies that U.S. forces were gathered nearby. These methods of confusion and deception became known as "special effects."

I don't make such a bad looking general, eh?

OPERATION BRITTANY: DEADLY SHOW AT BREST

In mid-August 1944, the Allies broke out of Normandy. Accompanied by the Ghost Army, U.S. forces headed for the port city of Brest on the western tip of France.

Their mission was to seize the city, which was heavily fortified by the Germans.

Controlling the port would allow the Allies to ship in supplies and equipment for the fight against Germany.

I feel like a drowned rat. But with the 6th Armored Division in action elsewhere, this mission is critical.

Yep, we need to do a good job imitating the 6th. If we do, the Germans will believe we have a greater fighting force than we really have.

Which will force them to surrender--I hope.

And if they don't, it's going to be one heckuva bloody fight to take Brest by force.

By this time, the Ghost Army's sonic unit had arrived in France. During training, technicians had recorded the sounds of moving tanks, trucks, and jeeps. They also recorded many other sounds of military activity, including soldiers' voices.

Not a single sound was overlooked. Any sound that could contribute to a successful deception was recorded.

I want a cleaner take on the tank backing up. Tell the driver we need to try it again.

During a mission, the recordings were played through huge speakers mounted on M-3 half-track armored carriers.

At Brest, half-tracks were positioned along a road leading into the city. The soldiers played the various recordings to convince the Germans of nearby Allied activity.

Set up down the road about a half-mile.

We don't want the Germans to miss this.

The Ghost Army also set up dozens of dummy tanks and guns to simulate a battalion of U.S. artillery forces.

The nighttime work was dangerous. German forces had placed mines along the roads into Brest. And German troops could attack at any moment.

If this works, we'll draw the German's fire toward the dummy tanks and guns. That will help the real forces do their job.

Hmm, there's a German observer in that church tower. I'll have to keep an eye on the fake tanks' gun barrels.

If they deflate and sag, the Germans will know what we're up to by morning. We've got to keep them inflated all night.

Over three nights, enemy shells pounded the dummy positions. The real U.S. forces received none.

Not a single member of the Ghost Army was injured or killed in the attacks. The luck of the Ghost Army was holding out.

But the Allies had underestimated the German forces at Brest. Rather than 16,000 troops, nearly 40,000 German soldiers held the city. The Germans were well stocked with weapons, ammunition, and supplies. General Hermann-Bernhard Ramcke commanded Germany's forces.

The powerful 6th Armored Division is here. But we won't surrender.

I have orders to fight to the last man, and I am determined to carry them out.

On August 25, the Ghost Army had earlier begun a decoy mission on a main road into Brest. Convinced it was a real attack, German artillery opened fire on the fake unit.

KRA-DOOM

KRA-DOOM

But because of miscommunication, a battalion of real U.S. tanks attacked down the same road at the same time.

Sadly, many U.S. tanks and lives were lost in the fighting.

The Ghost Army pulled out of Brest two days later on August 27 . . .

We didn't bluff the Germans into surrendering. But at least we kept them from breaking out of the city. We put on a good show.

Yeah, but maybe it was too good of a show. I can't believe we messed up the other day. So many of our own boys were lost.

We need to coordinate better with every unit we work with in the future. I never want to cause casualties to our own boys again.

Yeah, it was horrible. There's no excuse for that kind of deadly mistake.

Despite the tragedy, the Ghost Army commanders were pleased with the unit's performance in Operation Brittany.

Despite the previous mistakes, General Ramcke had fallen for the Ghost Army's deception. As he prepared for an attack by the fake 6th Armored Division, the real forces pounced on Brest from a different direction.

After weeks of brutal house-to-house combat, the Germans surrendered to Allied forces on September 19.

However, during the fighting the Germans had purposely destroyed the port. It was useless to the Allies.

THE LONG, BRUTAL WINTER

The Allied forces continued their relentless advance toward Germany. On August 25, 1944, Allied troops liberated Paris, France, putting an end to four years of German occupation.

When the Ghost Army arrived in Paris, they were able to unwind for the first time in months. The men enjoyed the excitement and culture offered by the famed City of Lights.

Artists in the Ghost Army passed the time by sketching and painting the sites of Paris.

The men toured famous landmarks and relaxed in nightclubs and music halls.

But the fun didn't last long.

We've got orders to move out immediately. General Patton's Third Army needs us more than ever.

For the next several weeks, the Ghost Army followed General Patton's Third Army as it raced toward the German border. Deception operations were conducted in France, Luxembourg, and Belgium. By now, each mission drew enemy artillery fire.

Keep it moving--we've got hours of work ahead of us!

The winter that year was the coldest in recent memory. The Ghost Army troops worked round-the-clock in bitter, freezing weather.

In mid-December, the Germans launched a massive attack on the Allies in eastern Belgium. Called the Battle of the Bulge, the attack threatened to break the Allied line as it advanced on Germany.

The Ghost Army was sent back to Luxembourg to avoid being captured by the Germans.

Allied units rushed to join the fight at the Bulge. But several gaps remained in the line approaching Germany. The Ghost Army was ordered to fill the gaps at the German-held city of Metz, in northeastern France.

Make it look believable, guys! We've got to keep the Germans from breaking out and attacking General Patton from the rear!

The unit used their full range of skills at Metz—visual, sonic, and radio deception.

Two parts of Operation Metz featured special effects only. The soldiers used shoulder patches, bumper designs, and road signs to fake the presence of the 87th and 90th Infantry Divisions.

The enemy is nearby. But you're safe as long as the 90th remains in the village.

90th INF DIV.

Both deceptions worked perfectly. The German forces in Metz believed they faced an enormous Allied force. They decided not to attack the Allied line. Meanwhile, the real 87th and 90th Infantry Divisions were pounding the enemy at the Bulge.

January 7, 1945. As Operation Metz drew to a close, sonic crew truck driver Chet Pelliccioni built a fire on top of a pile of snow. He wanted to keep himself and his comrades warm.

Ch–Chet!!

BLAM!

AAAAGGH!

Without warning, the fire exploded. A German hand grenade had been covered by the snow.

For months the Ghost Army had operated dangerously close to German tank and infantry units. They had escaped blistering artillery fire with no casualties. But now the first Ghost Army soldier was killed by simply lighting a campfire.

The luck of the Ghost Army had finally run out.

The Ghost Army had little time to grieve for their fallen comrade. Though the Allies won the Battle of the Bulge in late January, the war raged on.

The unit then set off on their most critical mission yet—Operation Viersen. It would be a dangerous crossing of the Rhine River directly into the heartland of Germany.

21

THE GREATEST ILLUSION OF ALL

By early March 1945, the Allies prepared to cross the Rhine River. The Germans hoped to use the waterway for defense, and then mount a fierce attack to drive back the invaders.

Keep 'em moving. We musn't keep the Nazis waiting!

More than 1 million Allied soldiers were set to make the crossing. It would be the largest assault by water since the landings on D-Day.

If we pull this off, it'll be the beginning of the end for the Nazis.

Two armies will make the assault: the 21st Army Group under British general Bernard Montgomery and the American 9th Army.

I need your Special Troops to pull out all the stops on this mission, Lieutenant Colonel Truly. They'll pretend to be the 9th Army and stage a deception at Viersen, about ten miles south of the actual crossings.

We need to make the Germans believe we're crossing at Viersen. Thousands of lives depend on your men's success.

The Ghost Army is at peak efficiency, General Simpson. We've learned plenty from all our missions. We won't let you down.

The Ghost Army prepared for their greatest deception at a furious pace.

You'll need to inflate those tanks faster than that, soldier!

In all, nearly 620 fake tanks, trucks, and artillery were used in the mission.

Dummy tanks and real equipment were set up in forests and small towns. The Ghost Army created the illusion of a massive military build-up.

Smoke screens were used to make the Germans think the Allies were trying to hide real military activity.

The men set up makeshift landing fields to improve the illusion. Inflatable observation planes looked like the real thing.

If I didn't know better, I'd swear I could fly that fake plane!

The sonic unit played sounds of trucks and jeeps driving around. The soldiers also played sounds of portable bridges being built.

Crank it up! They've got to get the message loud and clear.

Dozens of German planes flew over Viersen to see what the Allies were up to.

Yah, the area is filled with enemy guns and equipment. The 9th Army is surely here.

Convinced the Allies were just across the river at Viersen, the Germans began pouring in gunfire.

KA-KROOM!

KA-KROOM!

For five nights, the Germans pounded the Ghost Army positions. Not a single man was injured.

Patch 'em up fast and reinflate 'em! Drag off the ones we can't fix.

The Ghost Army also coordinated with real Allied forces for their mission. Elements of the 9th Army flew missions over a fake attack area across the river to complete the illusion.

I hope the Germans are buying into our scheme. If they don't, a lot of our troops will be killed trying to cross the river to the north.

March 22, 1945. On the eve of the river crossing, Allied leaders met near the real attack zone to watch the assault. Supreme Allied Commander Dwight D. Eisenhower, British Prime Minister Winston Churchill, and General Montgomery attended the meeting.

Have we fooled the enemy, General Eisenhower?

We'll soon find out, Prime Minister. We don't know how many Germans are waiting on the other side of the river.

If we meet little resistance, we'll know their main forces remained at Viersen.

On March 23, the Allies began the dangerous crossing of the Rhine River. They watched nervously, anticipating the deadly reception they might face on the opposite side.

Amazingly, they met little resistance. The crossings took the enemy completely by surprise. Only 31 U.S. soldiers were killed—thousands less than expected.

The 1,100 men of the Ghost Army had fooled the Germans into thinking they were the 30,000 soldiers of the 9th Army.

Operation Viersen would be the Ghost Army's last, most important, and most successful mission of the war.

By the end of March, tens of thousands of Allied troops were battling enemy forces across Germany.

Germany surrendered on May 7, 1945. After six bloody years, the war in Europe was finally over.

HISTORY'S INCREDIBLE DECEIVERS

After Germany's surrender, the Ghost Army spent a few weeks helping guard refugee camps in Europe.

In late June 1945, the men of the Ghost Army returned to America aboard U.S. Navy transport ships.

The men were told to never speak about the work of the Ghost Army.

23rd Headquarters
Special Troops
Activated January 1944
Deactivated September 1945

TOP SECRET

The records of the unit were kept secret by the Army for more than 40 years. Some of its activities remain classified to the present day.

By the 1990s magazines and newspaper articles began to reveal the remarkable story of the Special Troops.

The accomplishments of the Ghost Army—the army that never fired a shot—were finally written into the pages of history.

Many members of the Ghost Army went on to have great success after the war.

Ellsworth Kelly became a renowned painter and sculptor whose works greatly influenced American art.

Art Kane was a successful photographer who created memorable portraits of famous musicians.

Bill Blass became a world-famous fashion designer.

Arthur Singer became a world-famous wildlife artist who created many illustrations for magazines, books, and encyclopedias.

Experts estimate that the Ghost Army saved as many as 40,000 Allied lives.

"Each time German divisions were frozen in place, it meant that they were not killing Americans elsewhere," wrote journalist Jack Kneece.

The men of the 23rd Headquarters Special Troops were skilled, brave, and resourceful. They created and waged a unique form of warfare, unlike any seen on a battlefield before.

The members of the U.S. Ghost Army were history's greatest masters of illusion.

GLOSSARY

Allies (AL-lyz)—the group of countries that fought against the Axis powers in World War II, including the United States, Great Britain, France, and the Soviet Union

battalion (buh-TAL-yuhn)—a large unit of armed forces

camouflage (KA-muh-flahzh)—coloring or covering that helps hide objects and people by making them look like their surroundings

comrade (KOM-rad)—a good friend or someone you fight with in battle

decoy (DEE-koi)—an object or action used to lure animals or people to a desired location

half-track (HAF-trak)—a military vehicle with wheels at the front and tanklike tracks at the rear

impersonate (im-PUR-suh-nayt)—to pretend to be someone else

intercept (in-tur-SEPT)—to secretly receive a communication, especially one intended for an enemy

Morse code (MORSS KODE)—a method of sending messages by radio using a series of long and short clicks

simulate (SIM-yoo-layt)—to recreate objects or locations that look like the real thing

sonic (SON-ik)—having to do with sound waves

READ MORE

Alberti, Enigma. *Victor Dowd and the World War II Ghost Army.* Spy on History. New York: Workman Publishing, 2018.

Bearce, Stephanie. *World War II: Spies, Secret Missions, and Hidden Facts from World War II.* Top Secret Files. Waco, TX: Prufrock Press, Inc., 2015.

Williams, Brian. *World War II: Visual Encyclopedia.* New York: DK Publishing, 2015.

CRITICAL THINKING QUESTIONS

- The U.S. Ghost Army were masters of illusion more than 70 years ago. But modern armies use many high-tech drones and observation planes. Do you think the Ghost Army would succeed in their missions today? Explain your answer.

- Imagine that you're a member of the U.S. Ghost Army. Create a journal describing your experiences during the war. What is it like to be in the middle of a combat zone? What kind of work do you do to help your team succeed in its missions?

- The book you're holding is written in a graphic novel, or comic-book, style. The artwork in the book helps to tell the story. List some of the ways you think this graphic novel helped you learn more about the U.S. Ghost Army and the work it did to help win World War II.

INTERNET SITES

D-Day: The Invasion of Normandy
https://www.ducksters.com/history/world_war_ii/d-day_invasion_of_
normandy.php

The Ghost Army
https://www.warhistoryonline.com/featured/the-ghost-army-how-an-
army-of-artists-helped-win-world-war-ii.html

Ghost Army Legacy Project
http://www.ghostarmylegacyproject.org/overview.html

INDEX